THE ARGUMENT

OF

WM. P. DUVAL,

ON

CLAIM OF THE CITIZENS OF TEXAS

FOR

COMPENSATION FOR THE PROPERTY TAKEN FROM THEM BY THE CAMANCHE INDIANS, SINCE THE ANNEXATION OF THAT STATE TO THE UNITED STATES.

WASHINGTON:
PRINTED BY GOGGIN & SAUNDERS.

1852.

ARGUMENT.

To the Committee of Indian Affairs *of the House of Representatives, who have in charge the petition of Messrs.* Berry, Cox, Williams, Lee, and others, *citizens of the State of Texas, praying Congress to indemnify them for property taken or destroyed by the Camanches and other tribes of Indians, on the borders of the white settlements of said State, since its annexation to the United States:*

Gentlemen: In presenting the claims above referred to, others of a like nature will necessarily fall within the general principles that govern the whole class of Indian spoliations, unless peculiar circumstances may vary the equity of some of the claimants. It has often been asserted that the Congress of the United States do not hold the nation bound by justice or policy to make good the losses sustained by her citizens in a war with a foreign power. This, as a general rule, may be admitted, yet in many instances Congress has paid for property taken or destroyed by the enemy during our last war with Great Britain, *not in the use or service* of the United States, or *occupied by our military*, or destroyed by *order of the officer in command.* A list of cases, with the proper references, is hereunto appended. It was then the uniform practice of Congress, in every act passed granting compensation to persons for the destruction of property, when the same was destroyed by order of the commanding officer, or destroyed by the enemy while in the use or occupation of the military, to set forth in the *law* the fact; and a review of the several acts of Congress, for this kind of indemnity, will show their uniformity in this particular. In all other cases, where compensation was granted by Congress for property taken or destroyed in the war with Great Britain, the act of Congress simply states, the property was taken or destroyed by the *British troops* during the war of 1812, and in the years 1812, 1814, or 1815.

Waiving all discussion as to the right of our citizens to indemnity for losses incurred in a war with a foreign enemy, the Indian tribes within the limits of the United States stand on a principle wholly "different, perhaps unlike that of any two people in existence." "In general, nations not owing a common allegiance are foreign to each other: the term *foreign nation* is with strict propriety applicable by either to the other. But in the relation of the Indians to the United States, this is marked by peculiar and cardinal distinctions, which exist nowhere else." (*Cherokee Nation* vs. *State of Georgia.* See 5 *Peters' Reports.*) "Those Indian tribes which reside within the acknowledged boundaries of the United States cannot with strict accuracy be denominated *foreign nations.* They occupy a territory to which we assert a title independent of their will, which must take effect, in point of possession, when their right of possession ceases. Meanwhile they are in a state of pupilage: their relation to the United States resembles that of a *ward* to his *guardian.* They look to our Government for protection, rely upon its kindness and its power, appeal to it for relief to their wants, and address the President as their *Great Father.*" (5 *Peters' Reports, same case.*) If the United States chooses to become guardian to the Indians, does it exclude guardianship of its own citizens? Does the protection of the one necessarily exclude the other? It seems but just that the guardian should protect both wards, as he holds in truth the estates of both. He should see each held accountable to the other for their losses. If it should be said that the Indians have no estate to answer the demands of justice, he ought to give some account of the millions of acres that he holds as trustee for the Indian; and is daily receiving the proceeds, *as residuary legatee of his own creation,* much against the will of his *red ward.*

The manner and mode of proceeding pointed out by the act of Congress of the 30th March, 1802, entitled "An act to regulate trade and intercourse with the Indian tribes, and to preserve peace on the frontier," is so clogged with conditions and provisoes, which in many instances cannot be complied with, from the very nature of the country, and the wandering life of the Indians, (they having no permanent home, and not cultivating the soil,) without annuities, and destitute of means to indemnify the party for any loss or damage to his property. The act of 1802 is a *dead letter*, so far as the indemnity to our citizens for Indian depredations is concerned. Its complicacy defeats its own object, as much so as if it had been designed to prevent any payment for such losses.

It has been heretofore stated in Congress that Texas should have run a line through her territory, and placed the Camanche tribes over that line, so that the War Department might establish its posts on such line permanently, and thus keep the Indians out of our settlements; and not having made such line of division, Texas or her people are to be left to the mercy of the savages, and must suffer for the omission. In answer to this, I say that Texas is more justly entitled to claim of the United States indemnity for her citizens than any other State in the Union: *First.* Because she acceded to all the demands made on her by the articles or resolutions admitting her into the Union. *Second.* The United States did not require Texas to lay off and appropriate territory within her limits, for the use of the Indians. Why then should this new demand be urged as a reason, that her citizens should not be indemnified for their property plundered by the *Indians?* Had Congress requested, in the resolutions passed for the admission of Texas, that such a line should be run, and a portion of her unsettled lands set apart for a limited time, for the use and occupancy of the Indians, no doubt it would have been acceded to. But so far from doing this, or giving protection to the people of Texas, Congress required the State to deliver up all of her arms, posts, arsenals, and munitions of war, leaving the State at the mercy of the Indians, utterly disarmed. To a thinking mind, it must seem extraordinary that a new country, with vast numbers of daring warriors hovering about her settlements, and with a border of many hundred miles, should have been required to surrender the arms so necessary to their security and defence. Texas, up to the time of her admission into the Union, would have greatly preferred to retain her arms, &c., by a surrender of a portion of her unsettled wild lands, for the temporary occupation of the Indians.

It has been offered as an excuse for the want of that efficient protection which Texas since her annexation has never received, but which the Congress of the United States is by duty and the Constitution bound to give, that the United States own no land in the limits of Texas.

The Constitution grants to Congress the exclusive power to regulate the Indian tribes in their intercourse and trade, and to preserve peace on the frontier. What soil did the United States own in New York, North Carolina, Georgia, and other States, where the Indians remained? Georgia was the only State that, by compact with the United States, agreed to permit the Indians within her borders to remain for a reasonable time, until the General Government could conveniently remove them; and after most unreasonable delay, that State was forced to adopt decided action before the Indians were removed from her soil.

Whatever opinion was entertained by any department of the General Government as to the necessity of the United States having control over the soil in any State, in order to give the citizens prompt and efficient protection against the Indians, surely the act of Congress, approved 29th December, 1845, should put to rest this pretence, as the act declares "all the laws of the United States extend to and over, and are to have full force and effect in, the State of Texas.

It may be asked with reason and propriety, why the United States, out of all her millions of acres lying north and west, on the borders of Texas, have not furnished land for the tribes of *Camanches?* The vast plains and rich pastures unocccupied by a white man is the very country best suited to these Arabs of the plains, not inferior to the best horsemen in the world. Why, then, should the United States expect Texas to yield her lands to the savages? Is this any part of her agreement? And shall it be urged, under these circumstances, that a people disarmed by the General Government, without the means of protecting their lives or property, and fallen, as many of them have, under the fury of the savage, should receive no indemnity for the loss of almost all they possessed?

In the treaty made by the United States with the Indians in Georgia, a stipulation was made that a certain sum should be paid to the citizens of that State as indemnity for losses sustained by her citizens from the Indians within her limits, out of the money the Indians were to receive for surrendering their possessions and removing west of the Mississippi. I believe the amount thus applied did not by any means liquidate and pay the just sum due the citizens for their losses. The act of Congress which proposes to secure to the citizens of the United States indemnity for Indian depredations, has proved a failure, except when enforced by some treaty made with the Indians. If this act had been fairly and justly executed, it would have been wise economy saving the lives of thousands of our citizens, and millions that have been expended in suppressing Indian hostilities. Whenever the General Government complies with its laws, no citizen will seek to redress his wrongs by strong hand, or seek reprisals or revenge for his losses. It is certain that our citizens will attempt to redress the wrongs inflicted by the Indians, if the Government will not. It is to the interest of the United States to pay for the property taken or destroyed by the savages, rather than incur the expense of hostilities with them. Humanity to our own citizens demand this course, as it does for the protection and preservation of the unfortunate *red race.* Your Indian wars have cost the nation millions more than if every citizen had received *full compensation* for all the property taken or destroyed by the Indians since our Government was established, to say nothing of the loss of so many lives sacrificed in these conflicts.

The treaty made with the various bands or nations of the Camanches, on the 5th day of May, 1846, in Robertson county, in the State of Texas, by the commissioners on the part of the United States, contains a stipulation in the 7th article, "that, as these bands or nations are in the practice of stealing horses from our citizens, and if persisted in, it cannot fail to involve the United States and the Indians in endless strife, it is therefore agreed that it shall be put an *entire stop* to on both sides." These Indians prefer to eat horses and buffaloes, and live entirely on meat. They are wandering over the plains, have no regular habitations, and raise no corn: to expect them to return the horses they steal, is about as reasonable as to suppose a starving man would give up his dinner.

Unless the United States can locate these Indians, and induce them to cultivate the soil, they will never remember the agreement not to steal horses, or, if stolen, to return them. Unless the United States will furnish them *rations*, all the horses *they steal* will be made into beef. It is this passion or appetite for horse-flesh that has occasioned so many horses to be stolen from the citizens of Texas, as they answer the double purpose of war horses and rounds of beef. I assure the committee that the Camanches must be either *destroyed* or *fed;* and Congress will exercise its wisdom and humanity, if it desires to prevent their extermination.

It may be said, that if the Indians are unable to pay for the property, the law promises, under certain conditions, (after a *year's delay*,) the United States is then to pay for it. If the claimant is to come here for relief, his claim must be very large indeed if he did not eat it out long before he could get a law passed in his favor. If he apply to the proper department to get pay for his losses, however full and clear the evidence might be, he would be informed that Congress must make the appropriation before his claim could be paid, for no such fund embracing his case had been or ever was set apart for this object. The result of all this injustice is, the injured citizen looks to his rifle to square his account. Hence the frequency of our Indian hostilities, and the millions spent by way of economizing a few thousand dollars.

The customs and habits of the Camanches, and their manner of warfare, should claim the attention of the committee, as a knowledge of these will show the equity of the cases of the Texas claimants. In three material points the Camanches differ from all other Indian tribes known to us.

First. They always act as mounted men, and better or more fearless riders are not to be found. Their horses are well trained, and they are enabled in quick time to rush into our settlements, (generally in the night, when the frontier inhabitants are sleeping,) and, when there is no moon, silently and adroitly they are enabled to plunder and carry off the horses and mules before daylight. Thus all the animals fit for the saddle are carried away, leaving the inhabitants afoot and unable to pursue the Indians with any hope of overtaking them. All the tribes, except those on the great western prairies, go to war on foot.

Second. The Camanches use no bread, and know nothing of it except as they see it in our settlements. They subsist entirely on the flesh of the buffalo and horse—the first daily becoming more scarce.

Third. The Camanches, contrary to the habits of all other Indian tribes, invariably violate their female captives. These facts are notorious to the citizens of Texas, and they have engendered the most deadly hostility against this wild and numerous nation. If their wives and daughters are thus treated, and their property thus plundered, finding no redress here, it requires no prophet to foretell, their rifles will clear and square the account with these Camanches, and the United States will have at last, and at great expense, to turn their arms against these savages.

The United States are munificent to the new States, and to many public institutions. To railroads, canals, &c., more than twenty millions of acres of the public domain have been granted by Congress. They have granted, too, a large amount of land, as pre-emptions to actual settlers; but these, being generally poor, have to pay the minimum price for the lands they occupy. This may be wise and prudent, as it brings large tracts of country into cultivation, increasing the value of the lands retained by the United States, and enabling the enterprising and laboring emigrant to find a home and comfort for his family, placing them in a position to acquire independence, and often in a few years wealth. These are generally located in peace, and secured from the inroads of the Indian.

Amidst all this liberality, who has thought or felt for the frontier man, for the bold and daring pioneer? These seem to be forgotten; yes, these brave and fearless men, who have in so many instances, and under so many privations, won from the fierce warriors the wilderness and the waste, and created an empire, now occupied by many prosperous and happy millions of people, daily adding strength and wealth to the nation—they are neglected and forgotten. Who casts a thought on such humble and distant and obscure sons of the frontier? Will you let them fall, and be stripped of their little property? The great and magnificent march of this nation to dominion and power is so towering, these sons of obscurity are not noticed in our triumph and glory. We boast of laws and equity, and of our republican institutions, and, over all, our noble Constitution and impartial justice. We profess to protect the weak and poor against the powerful and wealthy. Shall these claimants find all these are merely themes for our political orators—declamation to adorn some fourth of July oration? It is hoped not, and that Congress will practise what the Constitution and justice demand. The rich and powerful in all nations have and will protect themselves. It is the poor and humble who want the protection of the Government; and if they have it not, constitutional protection is a mere promise, broken as it is uttered.

You give away to railroads, held now and to be owned hereafter by wealthy stockholders, millions of acres of the domain, made valuable to the nation by the daring and gallantry of the untiring pioneer; yet none of all these lands, thus acquired, have been disposed of to pay for the destruction or loss of their property by the Indians; and shall these men, when they petition Congress for some compensation, be told, "Look to the act of the 30th of March, 1802, and the subsequent laws of Congress, for redress?—laws which have never been executed by the Government, except only when enforced by some treaty stipulation, or by special applications directly to Congress.

WM. P. DUVAL,
Attorney in fact for the Claimants.

APPENDIX.

Cases in which Congress paid for the capture or destruction of property in the late war with Great Britain, when the same was not in the use or occupancy of the United States or her troops, nor destroyed by the orders of the officers in command.

An act for the relief of Joseph McNiel.—(See Little & Brown Statutes at Large, containing Laws of the United States, published in 1819, vol 6, page 259.)

An act for the relief of William Henderson, for the value of his property destroyed by the enemy in the late war with Great Britain.—(Vol. 6, p. 268.)

An act for the relief of the heirs of Edward McCarty, deceased, for property destroyed by the enemy, during the invasion of Louisiana by the British troops during the late war.—(Vol. 6, page 270.)

An act for the relief of Solomon Prevost, for losses sustained by him, during the invasion of Louisiana by the British troops, during the years 1814 and 1815.—(Vol. 6, page 273.)

An act for the relief of John Pettel, for the destruction of his buildings and other property, during the invasion of New Orleans by the British troops in the winter of 1814 and 1815.—(Vol. 6, page 277.)

An for the relief of the legal representatives of John Guest, deceased, for a house and brick office burnt in the town of Havre de Grace, in the State of Maryland, in the year 1813, by the British troops.—(Vol. 6, page 400.)

An act for the relief of Wm. Flood.—(Vol. 6, page 163.)

An act for the relief of the representatives of Thomas Beacham, deceased, for a barn burnt in the State of Virginia, during the late war with Great Britain and her troops.—(Vol. 6, page 626.)

An act for the relief of the heirs of William Forbes, deceased, for property in certain houses destroyed in the late war by the British troops.—(Vol. 6, page 600.)

An act for the relief of Charles J. Catlett, for tobacco destroyed by the British or American troops, in the late war with Great Britain.—(Vol. 6, page 670.)

An act for the relief of David Kilbourn, for property destroyed on the northern frontier by the enemy during the late war with Great Britian.—(Vol. 6, page 690.)

An act for the relief of James L. Pattison, for a house and other property destroyed by the enemy during the late war with Great Britain.—(Vol. 6, page 709.)

An act for the relief of Wm. Eadus, for $2,000 for his house burnt by the British troops at Sodus, New York, in June, 1813.—(Vol. 6, page 710.)

An act for the relief of George Wallis, for the destruction of his cattle by the Indians—sum of $3,000, out of the annuities of Sac, Fox, and Iowa tribes.—(Vol. 6, page 913.)

There may be other cases of the same character as those above referred to; but the last mentioned case cannot avail the citizens of Texas, as the Camanche tribes are not allowed any annuities.

www.ingramcontent.com/pod-product-compliance
Lightning Source LLC
LaVergne TN
LVHW010833120826
845149LV00016B/1358

* 9 7 8 1 4 1 8 1 8 9 6 0 0 *